MW01537664

This Notebook Belongs To:

....

Published by Funable Journals
Copyright © 2019 by Funable Journals
All rights reserved. No part of this publication may be reproduced or distributed or transmitted in any form or by any means, electronic or mechanical, including, but not limited to, audio recordings, facsimiles, photocopying, or information storage and retrieval systems without explicit written permission from the author or publisher.

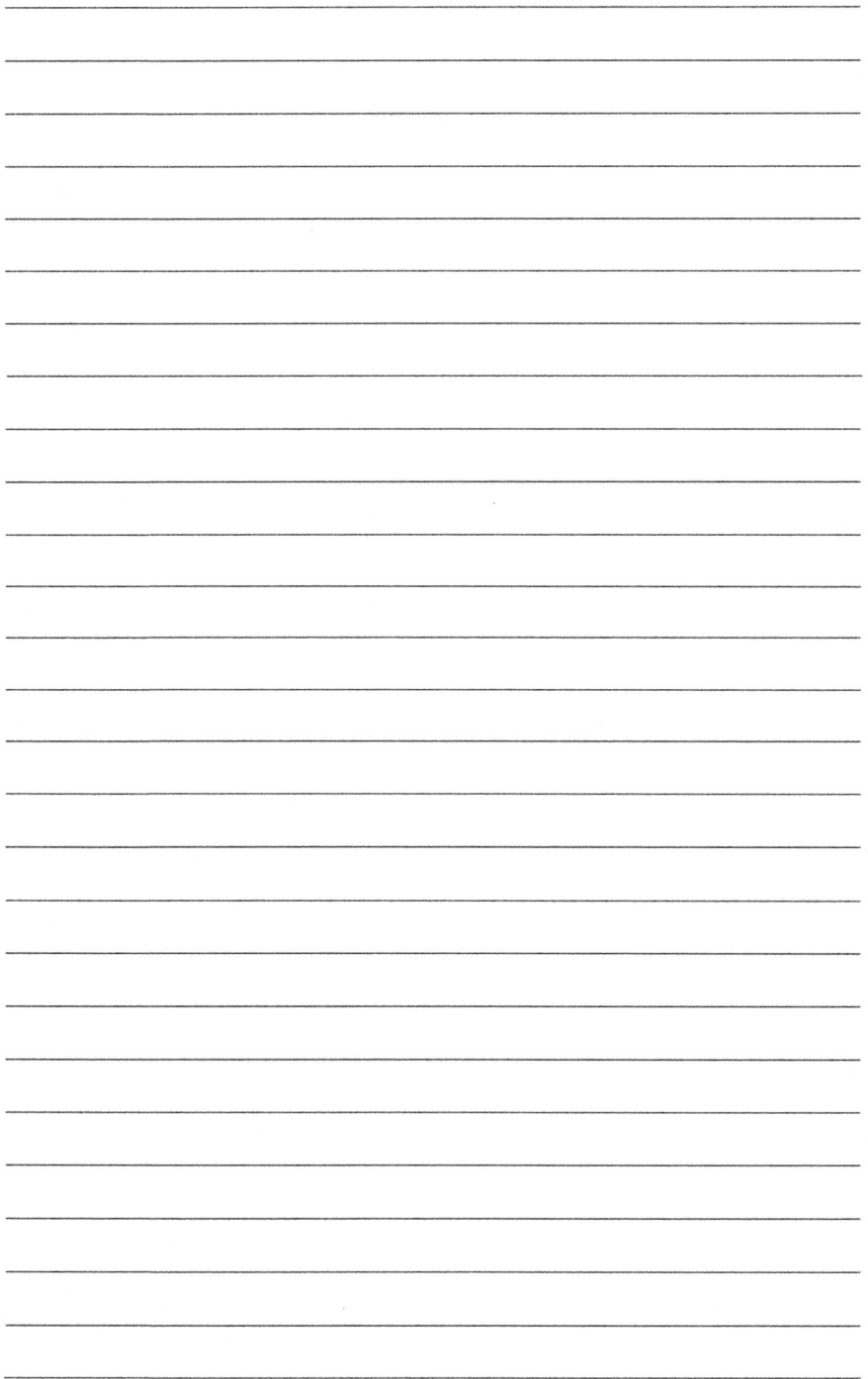

Made in the USA
Las Vegas, NV
04 December 2023

82123449R00069